HAPPINESS IS NOW

reflective writings of Yogi Amrit Desai

Kripalu Center for Yoga and Health, Lenox, Massachusettes

Second Edition
Second Printing, 1987
Copyright © 1982 by Kripalu Center

ISBN: 0-940258-03-X
Library of Congress Catalog Card Number 82-80489

Printed in the United States of America
by Kripalu Communications
Box 793, Lenox, MA 01240

—

CONTENTS

FOREWORD

It gives me great pleasure to introduce Yogi Amrit Desai (known by his students throughout the world as Gurudev, or "beloved teacher") and his work *Happiness is Now*. I first met him in January of 1976 when he came to Gainesville, Florida, to give a seminar on Kripalu Yoga. I was then Associate Professor of Physics and Electrical Engineering at the University of Florida. In Gurudev's presence I felt a powerful flow of energy which left me joyful, serene, and clear. From this experience, I had no doubt Gurudev was an unusual person! As I came to know him better, I was inspired by his qualities of character: his child-like purity and freshness, his natural humility and selflessness, and his consistent love for others. To me, he embodied virtues to which I aspired; I knew that the best way to acquire those qualities was to be around him. In 1978, I put my affairs in order, resigned my tenured professorship, and moved near him to learn from his life. That is one of the best decisions I ever made.

Others share my feelings; wherever he goes, before long hundreds of people are attracted to his presence. At Kripalu Center, each evening we set aside our daily activity and gather in the Chapel. Frequently Gurudev joins us. He enters, greeting us with sparkling eyes as he moves through the throng with a relaxed, powerful gait, a princely progress. He takes leadership of the music with the harmonium. Music fills the room, our minds, and our hearts until at last, fulfilling its expression, it becomes silent. We sit in meditation for a few minutes.

When Gurudev comes out of meditation, his first words reach us from another level of consciousness. They are notably unusual—soft, succinct, lucid. I often feel they come from my own higher self. They are spontaneous, yet cadenced. Gurudev wonders sometimes where such words come from, for they are thoughts he has never had before though they are expressions of his own experience.

When his teachings particularly touch me, I write them down. My habit is to edit them into free verse. Once I showed him a few edited selections. He liked them, so from time to time that autumn we would work on these selections. Gurudev would receive me with deep courtesy into his simple home. His small study looked out onto a little garden pond set among towering hardwoods. The morning sun glimmered through the trees, striking crystals in the window, splashing rainbow hues about the room.

Gurudev would go over each piece to see that the meaning was complete. We worked with delight, with total involvement, like two children at play. Sometimes a phrase would stimulate his keen insight, and suddenly he would be off around another corner of meaning, with me fast on his heels, as an unexpected pathway would open up and a whole new selection would be written. I remember most of all from those days his love, his joy, and the uplifting abundance of his creative energy. I am grateful for those hours.

The effect of Gurudev's teachings on me is profound. He once said,

> *"I have not come to teach you,*
> *but to love you;*
> *love itself will teach you."*

His love enables me to feel the meaning of his words with my heart, to recognize their beauty, truth, and harmony. They remind me of what I already know but have not put into words. They restore my soul's vision. They continue to give me fresh inspiration.

You can bring these words back to life by refilling them with the love with which they were spoken. One way is to read them aloud rather slowly, perhaps to a dear one. Listen as you read aloud; listen, and let these words speak to your soul.

When a phrase brings insight, that is the seed of a realization. It takes positive action on your part to cultivate the seed. The insight must be woven into the fabric of your daily life, and practiced. Through practice insight becomes knowledge.

Now take a deep breath and relax — let these introductory words fall away, and be still for a moment. It is in stillness that you can hear with your heart. When you are quiet, you are ready to begin.

Gray Ward, Ph.D.
(Gitananda)
Editor

December 29, 1986
Lenox, Massachusetts

These meditative writings
are to remind you
of what you already know.

The knowing is deep within.
You can feel it
when you are still.

Yours is the insight,
yours is the power
to become who you really are.

HAPPINESS IS NOW

HAPPINESS IS NOW

We live in the flow of time —
yesterday, today and tomorrow.
Tomorrow continuously becomes today
and today constantly becomes yesterday.

Yet we can only live in the present.
Yesterday is dead,
tomorrow isn't born.
Yesterday and tomorrow do not exist.
They only exist in our minds.
Yet, they do exist in our minds.
What exists in our minds affects us,
and the reality of the present
also affects us.

We are constantly preoccupied
by memories of yesterday
and fantasies of tomorrow.
Clouded by the conflict
of past memories and future dreams,
we cannot live in the present.

Possessed by the habit
of preparing for happiness tomorrow,
when tomorrow becomes today,
we're again preparing
for tomorrow,
the tomorrow that never comes.

We rarely enjoy what we are,
because part of us isn't home.
When we are in the moment,
we are in the home
of the eternal now.

Experience happens here and now.
The past and future are escapes
from true experience of life.
Our experience need be no different
than the way it is revealed
in every passing moment.

To project our dreams into the future
or to make them come true
is not the secret of life.
The secret is our ability to attend
to the experience of now.

LIVING THROUGH EXPERIENCE

Life is an experience,
not an explanation.
Life starts with experience.
All that we learn,
we learn by experience.

Explanations are only words
which point to experience.
In the absence of experience,
explanations are only information.
Explanations serve as maps;
they can point the way
to our destination,
but they cannot replace
the experience.

Empty explanations adopted
without matching experience
create emptiness in life.

All thinking diminishes experience.
In order to experience,
our minds must learn
to be silent.

We tend to believe that thought
enhances our experience.
Nothing distracts us more
from our experience
than the static
created by our thoughts.

In early childhood,
before our minds develop,
we learn by direct experience
and open interaction
more than we will learn
during the rest of our lives.
A child learns and grows
through experience
rather than through language.

Language expresses the experience,
but it cannot enhance the experience.
Thought creates an illusion of experience,
but it cannot enhance the experience.

As we watch a beautiful sunset,
we tend to interrupt our experience
and loudly exclaim:
"See the colors! How lovely they are!"
as if we could accentuate
the beauty of the sunset
by expressing it with words.

Our experience is subjective.
To express our experience
is to shift from within to without.
If we stop all expression of feelings
and simply feel what happens,
we can melt into what we feel.
Then we are one with the experience.

As we learn to live through experiences,
re-establishing a childlike openness,
more and more life begins to flow
through us.
We begin to experience the joys of life,
not as we think they should be,
but as they are.

BORROWED OPINIONS

Not one, but many
voices crowd our minds.
We think we are alone,
but many reside within.

Society conditions our minds.
Our thoughts are not our own.
Almost every thought we think,
we took from someone else.
Whether we feel we're good or no good,
what we like or don't like,
what we should or shouldn't be,
all of this
we absorbed from someone else.
We were not born with opinions,
they came from our mothers, our fathers,
our teachers, peers and priests.

When we live for years with opinions,
we think they are ours.
When fully conditioned to these thoughts,
we think we are these thoughts.
We defend our every opinion
as if we were the opinion.
When we drop borrowed opinions,
only ourselves remain.

Our minds are filters
which condition all incoming signals.
When we begin to see
life in its purest state,
without interpretations,
without likes and dislikes,
we experience
that which is.
Then we are in the presence of God.

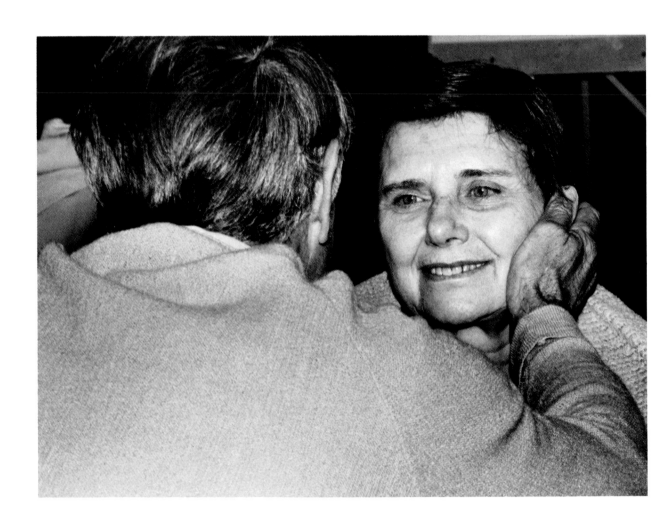

NO EXPECTATIONS

In our interactions,
the other is only a mirror
which again and again
brings us back to ourselves
and gives us a chance
to see who we really are.

We expect of the other
what we expect of ourselves.
Expectations of ourselves
deny who we are.
Denial of ourselves
gives rise to expectations
of the other person.

We only love the other
for who we expect them to be.
We expect the other
to fulfill our dreams.
We are really in love
with our own expectations.

As we slowly accept
who we really are,
we can truly love ourselves
and begin to love the other.

The more we drop expectations
in a loving relationship
the more true love blossoms.

SEE WITH WONDER, BE AS A CHILD _____

See the sweetness children have!
Their voices have a purity
because they have no purpose.
They are not afraid
that someone will think
they are foolish.
It doesn't matter to them.

When a child plays,
he plays for the sake of play.
The child is enchanted by the moment,
the timeless time,
the eternal now.
There is no purpose in the play,
nothing to change,
nothing to attain.

All that surrounds the child
is a source of wonder.
He walks and moves and looks
with great wonder in his eyes.

A child's eyes are ever empty,
like a mirror which reflects
only what is there.
All is mysterious,
surprising, fresh
and new.

We have forgotten now,
but one day we walked
with our eyes wide with wonder
feeling, "What's this?
What's that?
I never saw it before!"

When, like a child,
we experience life
with freshness, amazement,
and emptiness in our eyes,
then life itself
with all its mystery
will fulfill our deepest longings.

SEES OF DIVINE POTENTIAL

The body has wisdom
learned through eons
of slow evolution.
The body has wisdom,
but the mind has control.
The body's wisdom
can help us no more
than allowed by the mind
that controls its actions.

When body demands
some nourishing food,
the mind, addicted
to sensual pleasures,
provides empty devitalized food.

When the body says,
"That's enough!"
the mind,
ever greedy for pleasure
says "Go get some more!"

The restless mind
leads the body astray.
The wisdom of the body is lame
without the mind's cooperation.
The mind, like a step-ladder,
can be used to go up
or to go down.
The mind is both an asset
and a liability.

The mind is our friend,
as well as our foe.
When it follows the wisdom of the body,
it acts like a friend.
When it follows the dictates of ego,
it works as an enemy.

The mind is a victim
of the ego's insatiable greed.
The ego disturbs the mind
by greedily asking for fun.
It creates artificial demands
unrelated to bodily needs.

Ego agitates the mind
with thoughts of past and future,
which distract the mind
from attending
to the body's wisdom.
When the mind is blinded
by ego's lust and greed,
it works in conflict
with the body's wisdom.
The mind misguides the body
when it follows the foolish ego.

When mind performs in harmony
with the wisdom of the body,
the eternal wisdom
of the evolving universe
sprouts the seed
of divine potentials in man.

GRAVEN IMAGES

Because we do not love ourselves,
we imagine others
could not love us either.
How could others love us?
We have concealed ourselves
behind our glossy masks.

Our unconscious obsessive need
for approval and acceptance
has made us grave an image
which we hope
that others will love,
a mask ingeniously sculpted
for others to accept.

If we shrewdly succeed
in making others love us,
they have fallen in love
with the mask and not with us.
They fulfill the needs of our masks,
while our real needs go unfulfilled.

Two people in love
are often in love
with the mask of the other,
or with their own expectations.

Such love is a game we play
where love begins to die
as soon as it is born,
as all of our efforts go
to fulfill our false self-image.

If we are who we are without fear,
and drop our many masks,
our honesty makes us transparent.
The light of our love shines forth
and touches the hearts of others.

Love begins
when we set aside
all of our masks.

WE ARE NOT OUR THOUGHTS

We create our world
by the thoughts we harbor.
Thoughts are subtle objects
that can harm or heal.
They can pierce and wound the heart
more than the spear
or the sword.
Thoughts may lead us to suicide
or to self-realization.
Invisible surely they are,
yet, visible are their effects.
Our thoughts are the forces
that mold our lives.

Only awareness can harness thoughts.
We must learn to be aware
of what thoughts we are creating,
and of what the causes are
of the thoughts we harbor.

Associations mold and manipulate our thoughts.
Let us be aware of
the inner nature of thoughts,
and see where they come from,
and where they would lead us.

We can consciously watch
the formation of a thought.
We can watch it come into form,
then pass and disappear,
like a bubble that's born
at the ocean bottom,
which gets bigger and bigger
as it rises to the surface
and pops—as it vanishes
into universal consciousness.

As we sit in the center of our being,
we can watch our thoughts
as they come and go.
We can watch the entire process
of the formation of every thought,
its growth and final dissolution.

We don't have to fight to change them,
just look at them.
We need not fight, defend or judge,
but simply sit and watch them pass by,
like people passing by our window.

We can learn to see the passing thoughts
clearly, objectively, without comment,
apart from all associations
arising from past conditioning.

Then we know
we are not our thoughts.

TRUTH IS A PRIVATE REALIZATION

Existence is,
independent of words,
independent of explanations.
Words can speak about the truth,
but cannot speak the truth.
Truth can neither be ensnared by thought,
nor rendered by words.

Truth can see but cannot speak;
falsehood can speak
but cannot see.
Falsehood is strident and logical;
truth is silent.

When words of truth are repeated,
the truth cannot be heard.
The truth has to be
directly perceived.
To talk about truth is one thing,
to realize truth is another.

The truth is a private realization.
Those who realize the truth
cannot tell it.
They can talk about it,
but cannot tell us
what they found.

Those who find truth,
find it in inner silence.
If we can be perfectly still,
in pure perception
with no thoughts,
in those moments
we can find truth.

WE CAN CHANGE OUR WORLD

Let us take a moment to be still,
and rest our awareness upon
some nearby plant,
or the sky, or a tree.

Let us be still, and feel
what is happening within.

Are the feelings
coming from the object,
or coming from within us?

Feeling is reflected to us
by our experience.

The effect of every object
is a reflection of our own
inner images.

All that ever happened to us
was an experience
that we created.

Somehow we believe
that objects
create our experience.

When we believe that objects
create our experience,
we become materialistic
and our journey outward begins.

When we realize
we give meaning
to all that happens to us,
our journey inward begins.
Materialists are so busy
changing the world outside them,
they ignore the world within.

We imagine that objects and places,
people and their behavior,
command our experience,
be it good or bad.

When we fail to admit and affirm
our own responsibility
for all our experiences
and blame or acclaim another,
we are giving away our freedom
to change ourselves
and to control our experience.

Our responsibility and freedom
go hand in hand.
When we take responsibility
for all our experiences
both pleasurable and painful,
we can change our world.

LOVE RETURNS TO ITS SOURCE

Love begins by either
giving or receiving,
we can start at either end.
Love continues to grow
when we willingly give
after we have received,
or willingly receive
after we have given.

The energy of love
completes the circuit.
When we give love,
we receive love.
Love returns to its source.

We seek love and fear love
at the very same time.
We are afraid to receive
the love of other people,
since we know our turn will come
to give love in return.

Until we give
we cannot receive.
As we give spontaneously,
we are free to receive.

Giving designed to control
is not real giving.
Such giving is not from love
and lacks the sweetness of love.

As we learn to freely give
all we seek from others,
without wanting any return,
we find we are served by serving.
Whoever helps others
receives help from God.

RENEWAL

*To meet a person today
with our opinion of yesterday,
is to expect them to act
as they did before.
However different they may be,
we overlook the change
and tend to react
guided by our memories.*

*To judge the other
through the eyes of the past,
deprives them of freedom
to change and to grow
in our interaction.*

*To allow another to grow
is to allow ourselves to grow.
To judge another
is to feel judged.
To practice rejection
is to project rejection
and feel rejected.
To look at others
with newness in our eyes
is to feel renewed.*

*The way to be with others
is to be wholly with them
as they are
in the moment.*

THE CHALICE OF GRATITUDE

Gratitude for what we have
allows the flow of grace
to fulfill our every action.
Gratefulness awakens
the reposing grace
concealed in every action,
whether sacred or profane.

If gratitude is absent,
even sacred acts
fail to grant their grace.
When we feel ungrateful
for what we have already,
and even crave for more,
in spite of all our efforts,
we fail to find fulfillment.

In greed we miss
the grace of being grateful.
In greed we miss
the experience of the grace
we already received.
Grace is received
in the chalice of gratitude.

The basis of all our grace
is the feeling of contentment
with all that we are
and all that we have.

The fulfillment
hidden in the moment
can only be revealed
when we are grateful
for what we have.

SUBTLE WALLS

Thoughts are things. They emerge,
exist like other things, and perishing,
pass on, swiftly coming and going.

Thoughts exist on a subtle plane,
made of invisible matter.
Because they are invisible,
they seem to be less real.
Yet their presence is far from subtle.
Thoughts are forcefully known
by their tangible effects.
An angry thought
hits us like a blow,
while a loving thought
leaves a pleasant glow.
Thought-forms have definite impact,
more so than solid forms.

Gross things have their forms as well,
composed of grosser matter,
which we can easily see.
Gross things are slow to change,
and are readily controlled.

This world is a world of forms,
gross as well as subtle—
forms we can possess
forms that can possess us.

When we wisely use our possessions,
then they serve our needs.
When we fail to use them consciously,
our possessions rule our lives.
Unaware and unconscious,
we get caught in the world of forms.

The old familiar thought-patterns
we follow out of habit,
are as much our possessions
as our physical possessions.
We are conditioned by ideas
that we accepted from someone else.
We are posssessed by opinions
we have so long upheld
that we feel they are us.
We cling to our self-made prison,
fond of the filters of habit.

When our concepts become fixed,
those concepts become our prison.
The walls of our prison of concepts,
invisible as they are,
are stronger than any walls
man has ever built.
It is easy to escape
from external walls.
It is hard to escape
from the self-created prison
of concepts that limit our lives.
The confinement of those subtle walls
can indeed be broken
as we awaken
to our condition
and claim our freedom.

SEEING NEW IN THE OLD

Seeing freshly
comes from inner change.
Rather than seeking newness,
we only need to see newness
lying unnoticed around us.

Change can come in two different ways;
we can change the world around us,
or we can change the way we see it
by changing the world within.

When we change the world around us,
the newness quickly fades.
Our desires for change
make external change obsolete
before it is ready to change
in its natural rhythm.
No amount of newness
(which depends upon outer change)
will ever satisfy
our search for new and better
and remain forever new.

Seeking the new is one way,
seeing the new is another.
When we see the new
right within the old,
we are transformed from within
by our change of perception.
One fruit of inner growth,
of unfolding inner beauty,
is that the newness is revealed
in the old as well as the new.

We need to
forget how it was
and see how it is.

THE PROVINCE OF FAITH _____

Knowledge comes to us
in two distinctive ways.
one is from the known,
the other from the unknown.

Knowledge of the known
comes from the mind.
Knowledge of the unknown
comes from our faith.
The known
is the province of the mind.
The unknown is the province of faith.
Mind commands the known,
faith is open to the unknown.
Mind needs faith to extend the known,
and faith needs mind
to function in the world.

When we were children,
what we learned came to us
from the unknown.
The more our minds developed,
the less we let our knowledge
come from the unknown.
We seek security
and comfort in the known,
and resist and fear the unknown.

Experience of the unknown
is the root of our knowledge.
When we again attain
child-like openness,
we are able to shift
from known to unknown.

In our growth,
reformation happens
within the known.
The price of transformation
is the willingness
to move into the unknown.

The knowledge that comes
from the unknown
helps us live our lives
in greater fullness.

Knowledge from the known
gives the feeling of knowledge
but is not true knowledge.
It is rearrangement
of old facts.

If we want to go
on the inner journey,
like a child,
we need to understand
what mind cannot,
and accept experience
from the unknown
without explanation.

ENOUGH

All our striving
is to get enough,
which is forever endless.
Our desires for enough
are a bottomless well.
Throw in countless achievements,
they all disappear
without a trace.
They fail to fulfill
our demand for more.

Again and again we repeat,
"It is not enough. I want more."
Somehow we always believe
what we have is not enough.
We always want more than we have.

The aim of fulfilling desires
is to be free from their cravings.
When we are free from attachments
to demanding desires,
we are free from their compulsions.
Then our lives flow freely.

Satisfaction rarely comes
from getting what we want.
It usually comes to us
from enjoying what we have.
When we accept and enjoy
what we already have,
our needs are naturally provided
and we are fully satisfied.

LIFE IS LIMITLESS

What makes us think
our expectations
will be fulfilled?
Have they ever been?
Every event always turns out
differently from what we expect.
Expectations are never
fully fulfilled.

Our expectations come from our desires,
our cultural conditioning.
Life is not limited
by our conditioning.
Life is an unconditioned flow
of divine energy.
Life is consistent, dependable
and harmonious.
To experience life, we must accept
the uncertainties of tomorrow.

We must accept life as it is.

BURNING DESIRES

We carry within us
a clamoring chorus
of conflicting voices,
discordant desires,
each making demands for their fulfillment.
We feel responsible
for fulfilling the demands
of all our desires.

Desires have charms
and promise fulfillment.
Charming as they may seem,
they give birth to
the relentless irritation
of wanting more.
Desires, like itches,
keep coming back.
Feeding desires,
like scratching an itch,
gives brief relief,
but soon the itch turns to pain.

When we get what we want
and still feel unfulfilled;
when we perpetually desire more,
then accomplishment has failed
to fulfill its promise.
When desire gives birth
to desire for more,
more often,
in ever-increasing doses,
it is working against itself.
The desire adds fuel to the fires
of already burning desires.

It's not worth being caught
in attachments to desires
that leave us unfulfilled
and greedy for even more.

What is undesirable in desire
is our attachment to the desire.
When we are not attached,
we have the freedom to choose.
But when we are attached,
desire keeps growing
stronger and more blinding.

SEEING WHAT IS ALREADY THERE

When we work to fulfill
our selfish desires,
the world we see
is selfish, hostile
and lonely.

When our eyes are empty
of selfish seeking,
the world we see
is secure and serene.

The world
appears to be
as we are.

We are the instrument
and the player.
We are the cause
and effect.
We are the creator
and the creation.

Our experience of life
is an extension of
our inner attitudes.
As our attitudes change,
our lives begin to change.

There is no reality for us
apart from our values.
All that happens to us
happens through us.
We are the center
of our universe.

New and old,
good and bad,
are what we label
objects and incidents
of our world.

The world within is reflected
in the way we see
the world around us.

When we change,
our world changes.

"When we wear leather sandals,
our world is covered with leather."
What is within us
is reflected around us.

When we find our selves,
we have found it all.

The highest achievement
is when we begin to see
what is already there.

MESSENGERS OF TRUTH

This moment hides a message
that we need to hear.
It is ours when we're willing to risk
being aware of what's happening.

Every pain or problem has a message
of how to remove that pain.
Whenever we fail
to fearlessly face the pain or problem,
the message remains undelivered.

If fear prevents us
from decoding the message,
the pain keeps coming back
with increasing strength
until we respond.

When we learn the art of proper interpretation,
almost everything that happens
to us and around us
comes as a teaching to help us grow.
All experience, good or bad, of pleasure or pain,
hides a message planned for us.

To want our experience to be
other than what it is,
is to flee from the truth.
Neither pain nor pleasure are the truth;
they are the messengers of truth,
the truth that reveals who we are now.

What happens now
is the best that can happen.

To enter into the feeling of now,
to be willing to experience now,
we don't have to do anything.
We don't have to accomplish anything, only
just be, and all we want to achieve
will happen to us
and around us.
There are no techniques and nothing to do,
but simply feel what we're feeling right now.

To be open to our experience
is the gateway to freedom within.

Yogi Amrit Desai, known by his thousands of students as Gurudev (beloved teacher), is the founder and spiritual director of Kripalu Center. Internationally recognized as a master of yoga, Gurudev frequently leads seminars and speaks at conferences throughout North America, Europe and Asia, in addition to teaching in residence. Gurudev transmits to his listeners the essence of the ancient science of yoga—with its original depth and purity. He synthesizes it with current methods of holistic health and personal growth, and gives it universal appeal and relevance to modern life. No matter what his audience's background, Gurudev speaks directly to each person's heart and spirit—touching them with his boundless energy, sensitivity, humor, and love.

Married and the father of three children, Gurudev came to the United States from India in 1960, at the age of 28. He had been studying yoga since he was 16, with his revered Guru, Swami Shri Kripalvanandji (Bapuji). Gurudev began teaching yoga while attending the Philadelphia College of Art. After graduating, he became a textile designer and an award-winning watercolor artist; however, he left his successful art career to dedicate himself to teaching yoga. In 1966, Gurudev created the Yoga Society of Pennsylvania, which grew to be one of the largest yoga training organizations in the United States. In 1971, Gurudev established the original Kripalu Yoga Ashram, as a small retreat for himself and his students who wanted to live a contemplative lifestyle.

Since 1971, Kripalu has grown organically as Gurudev has continually extended his compassion and wisdom, welcoming more and more people who seek greater well-being, fulfillment, and inner peace. Gurudev's commitment to his own inner growth and to serving others selflessly is the inspiration for every program and service at Kripalu Center. His life is the model and the living spirit for the Kripalu experience.

KRIPALU CENTER

Located among the Berkshire mountains of western Massachusetts, Kripalu Center offers a variety of health holidays, educational programs and individual health services throughout the year. Our 200-member residential staff provides a setting which is uniquely supportive for bringing body, mind and spirit into the balance that is true health.

The basis of our approach is the ancient tradition of yoga and its principle that physical health is the foundation for emotional and spiritual development. Our programs and services combine time-tested yoga practices with more recently developed techniques in holistic health. They each provide experiential learning and first-hand knowledge of vibrant, comprehensive well-being along with practical methods for living a health-enhancing lifestyle at home.

Weekend, week-long and four-week programs focus on self-development through yoga, stress management, fitness, bodywork training and spiritual attunement. Our programs are excellent both for health professionals who want to expand the scope of their services and for individuals who, no matter what their background or occupation, want to derive more satisfaction and joy from their lives. Our guests can also individualize their visit, choosing from a wide range of classes, activities and facilities such as sauna, whirlpool, flotation tank and lakefront swimming.

For more information on our calendar of programs, write or call: **Kripalu Center, P.O. Box 793, Lenox, MA 01240, (413) 637-3280.**

OTHER WORKS BY YOGI AMRIT DESAI

Kripalu Yoga: Meditation in Motion
Kripalu Yoga: Meditation in Motion
    Book II, Focusing Inward
Working Miracles of Love
The Wisdom of the Body
Love Is an Awakening
Loving Each Other
Reflections of Love: a ten-year calendar
Journal of the Spirit